AND A YEAR WENT BY

AND A YEAR WENT BY

STEPHEN CLARK AND RICHARD MADDEN

ALAN SUTTON PUBLISHING LIMITED

First published in the United Kingdom in 1994
Alan Sutton Publishing Limited
Phoenix Mill · Far Thrupp · Stroud · Gloucestershire

First published in the United States of America in 1994
Alan Sutton Publishing Inc
83 Washington Street · Dover · NH 03820

British Library Cataloguing in Publication Data
A catalogue record for this book is available from the British Library

ISBN 0-7509-0540-9

Library of Congress Cataloging in Publication Data applied for

Designed by Alan Sutton Publishing Limited
based on the designs for the exhibition by
Roger Felton and David Gilligan of
Roger Felton Associates.

Typeset in 9/13 Gillsans.
Typesetting and origination by
Alan Sutton Publishing Limited.
Printed and bound in Great Britain by
Butler & Tanner Ltd, Frome and London

CONTENTS

Foreword

Acknowledgements

Introduction

FOREWORD

Modern life is a chaos of contradictions; it can be haphazard and boring, predictable and then unexpectedly horrifying. Is it ruled by mindless chance or a purpose we still simply cannot understand? In any event, it is hard to see shape or form in the muddle.

Religions and philosophies no longer help. To me, they seem quite inadequate to define the complex infinity that we face, their dogmas appear simple and inept.

I, and many like me, turn to art and the questing propositions of the artist. Art does not give answers; if it does, it makes propaganda. But it asks the right questions and experiencing it can help us formulate the right questions for ourselves. Perhaps that is why the art of the present and the art of the past have never been so popular – or necessary – as they are today. The great artist has, to his surprise, become the new high priest of our society.

Art gives form to chaos. The blank verse line of Shakespeare, the aria shaped by Mozart, or the two hours of cunningly juxtaposed images in a fine film, all regulate the chaos by subjecting it to form. It is our way of analysing the great mysteries.

Even the high jinks of Dada, where the form is always deliberately broken, end up being a vigorous form in themselves. And a phrase of music only eight or nine notes long, can be made happy or sad, tragic or comic, by the rhythm, pace, and harmonies that support it. But the form – the progression of notes – remains the same. Its mathematical rigour releases the possibilities of expression.

The form of this book is simplicity itself. Once a week a poet and a photographer met to contemplate something which fascinated them. The form is the year of meetings. On that, they based their creative forms – their verses and their pictures. Once more, the length of the line and the width of the lens released the human meaning at the very moment it was limiting it.

As the year went by, the artists found its progress a means of asking many questions, some private and some public. Finally, they made a subjective diary, of words and images.

I salute the stength and simplicity of their form and the rigour of their discipline. Theirs is an honest and surprising quest, full of many beauties. The form has released them and I believe it will do the same to anyone who gives time to this book. And it deserves time. The fragments make an enthralling whole which says a great deal about the '80s. It is a book of our time, both in its method and its mood.

Peter Hall

SIR PETER HALL

March 1994

ACKNOWLEDGEMENTS

An idea like the one which eventually materialised in this book needs encouragement – lots of it. In its final form the concept seems a perfectly acceptable one, obvious even. 'Twas not always so!

In the early days we often found our explanations of the project we had embarked upon met with blank incomprehension – to put it mildly! There were also times, after the fieldwork itself had been completed, when it seemed as if our efforts would never see the light of day. We owe a debt of gratitude to the select group of believers who kept alive our faith in the work. It is to your eternal credit that it has at last found the medium for which it was originally intended.

Photography, for obvious reasons, is very expensive to publish. We must, therefore, single out the names of those who sponsored us and contributed towards the publisher's costs in producing this book.

A big thankyou to: John Anstey, Marcel Berlins, Sacha Brooks, Tony & Anne Brooks, Guy Chapman, Kate Clanchy, Brian Clark, Don Clark, Maggie Clark, Brenda Cooper, Judy Daish, Anne Dawson, Steven Dexter, Jane Fawcett, Fiona Goble, Howard Goodall, Charles Hart, Peter Hicks, John Hollman, Imagination Ltd, Patricia McNaughton, Clare Patey, Cherry Potter, Jacqueline Rae, Peter Spafford, Jeni Williams.

There are also those without whom . . . Anne Dawson, Roger Felton, Friz, John Gibbens, Hannah Gordon, Susan Langford, John Langley, Jaqueline Mitchell, Mike Patey, Sue Raffael, Ayodele Ranson-Adisa, Peter Spafford. May your shadows never grow shorter.

INTRODUCTION

Time cannot pass without unfolding a story as it goes.

And a Year Went By is the story of a year told in poems and photographs. It is partly our story, partly the story of the seasons, of the year itself, but most importantly the story of the people whose lives we glimpsed.

Once a week we went to places or events that made us curious. Some had attracted our attention because they were in the news while others had been in the back of our minds for a long time but needed an 'excuse' to attend. There were also occasions when we wanted to explore more abstract ideas or feelings which were not tied to a particular time or place. The only principle that guided all our choices was curiosity. It not only seemed a good way to start, but perhaps it is the only way to start.

From the beginning we were very clear that neither the poem nor the photograph would merely explain or illustrate the other; only with the two working together would the full story unfold. In practice this meant sharing an experience but having the freedom to interpret it through the 'eye' of our own chosen art form. Later, when we came to put poem and photograph together, we discovered an even more complex and intriguing version of events, which enhanced the meaning of both.

We were always aware that at some stage one or both of us would not be available to do that week's 'photopoem'. As it turned out we were abroad, on separate assignments, for exactly the same eight week period during March and April. We decided that instead of a location or event we would agree a subject – Children, John McCarthy, A Lazy Day were three we chose – which we could then explore in our own way wherever we happened to find ourselves. These photopoems are extreme examples of us working independently and only seeing what it was we had created on our return. We didn't know what to expect but as it happened, thanks to the strength of the form, they include some of the work of which we are most proud.

The particular year, 1988/9, was chosen purely by chance. We had only just met and both of us were looking for a project that would allow us to explore the boundaries of our individual skills. As the project grew it also dawned on us that our subject matter was more than just the story of that particular year. As the weeks turned into months and the photopoems multiplied, we found that it was in fact turning out to be an exploration of what the 1980s had been all about.

The decade represented a significant change in many of the values that we had grown up with. Issues of democracy, personal freedom, attitudes to money, to race, to what it means to be part of society; all of these seemed to be changing. To have the opportunity to look at this process was serendipitous, challenging and ultimately very rewarding. To combine this with the changing fortunes of our personal lives and the rhythmic changes of the seasons themselves made for a heady brew.

It was a very exciting year; funny, bleak, frustrating and joyful. We hope you enjoy its story.

STEPHEN CLARK AND RICHARD MADDEN

THE PHOTOGRAPHS

The idea as I had first outlined it to Stephen was simple: one poem, one photograph, fifty-two weeks.

As far as we were aware, the form was unique (and still is). We had seen numerous examples of photography being used to illustrate poetry, particularly landscape photographs. This project, however, would be different. First there would be a story. Real events in real time. While we would, whenever possible, experience these events together, our responses would be subjective. Two different art forms, two different interpretations of the same event. The mystery ingredient we hoped would add a touch of magic would be the way in which we fused the two elements together.

In order to explain how I approached the photographic side of this book, I must first explain, albeit briefly, a few of my ideas about photography in general and my approach to the craft of photography in particular.

Even at its most basic level photography holds a deep fascination for me. If I am honest the photographs I look at most are snap-shots: badly composed, grainy and sometimes out of focus. But they are snap-shots of the people I love and they have captured something that I will never see again. What they do not have is feelings, ideas, shape or form, which is why, by and large, they are only of interest to me. The feelings that were present all those years ago, the ideas and dreams the people in those pictures held dear are as vivid in my mind as if they were yesterday. But to the dispassionate observer they have gone with the wind. It made me realise that for a photograph to have any universal appeal it had to fulfil different criteria.

As a documentary photographer there are certain basic necessities – compositional awareness, technical competence and discipline, among others. There is also the need to capture a moment that tells a story. A moment that communicates something of the before and after of which the resulting image is the pivotal point.

Perhaps even more important is the ability to 'see' the world the way a camera 'sees' it. During the course of everyday life we filter everything that we see through the complex web of thought and emotion we call our 'self'. A camera, however, sees only surface. This can be both liberating and restrictive. On the one hand the 'rational' rigidity with which we often interpret the shapes and textures in front of us can be removed, revealing a whole new world of visual possibilities. On the other hand all the 'inner' information of the photographer and his subject may be lost. Unless, of course, the possibilities of the first can be used to compensate for the apparent loss of the second. To use the hard exterior of shapes and forms to express something of what had gone on beneath the surface became my objective.

At the same time I also realised that the photographs I admired most were capable of expressing ideas. Often the surface subject matter of these pictures was disarmingly mundane. High drama, so often the domain of the news photographer, often relies more on its ability to shock the viewer rather than on subtlety of expression – an invitation to 'look at' rather than 'look into' the image. This area where the aesthetic of ideas and feelings was as important as form and content I came to think of as 'documentary art'. *The Photopoem, And a Year Went By* as it later came to be called, was the perfect vehicle to put some of these ideas into practice.

Let me give you an example. On the wet February evening we found ourselves in Piccadilly Circus I was immediately attracted by the reflections of the electronic hoardings on the wet pavement. On one level they made a strong graphic. I also felt that the pavement, the rain and the feet of the people passing by communicated something important about the values of Britain in the 1980s. In the darkroom I found I was able to extend this idea still further. The resulting image plays Escher-like tricks with perspective and portrays a mirror image of the ads whose logos still mysteriously read the right way round. For me this combined the *idea* of a looking-glass world of topsy-turvy materialist values with the *feeling* of a seductive shininess which was at the same time slippery, inhuman and depressing. For it to communicate effectively it also needs to be 'looked into' and not just 'looked at'.

From the beginning I did not set myself any rules as to how I would go about choosing the final image from the pages of contact prints. On some days the image in my viewfinder would seem so compelling that I had no doubt there and then that I had found what I was looking for: the image I took away from Smithfield Market for instance or the time I watched the farmyard cat at Lanner Vean farm basking in the early autumn sunshine.

On other days I could not be sure until later which scene would translate most effectively onto the page – Chelsea Flower Show for example or the party we gate-crashed in Oxford on Midsummer Day. Sometimes the answer was immediately obvious when I emerged from the darkroom. At other times I would find myself unable to choose. Often I would wait for Stephen to produce his poem and then examine my contact sheets with his work echoing through my mind.

There were also times when I felt that I had failed to produce a single image that was powerful enough. This happened on the occasion we went for an early morning walk through the grounds of Blenheim Palace in Oxfordshire. It was dark when we set out and the experience itself was full of atmosphere but more difficult than I had imagined to capture effectively in the half-light of a winter's morning. After reading Stephen's sonnet, I felt even more subdued. The negatives stayed a long time in a draw untouched.

In the end the answer arrived out of ideas we had developed in the meantime. The visual relationship of the poem with the photograph had become an increasingly important factor. We realised that each double page should be seen as a unified visual space within which anything and everything was possible. This helped ensure that I printed each photograph in the most appropriate shape for the image. Cropping is the primary process required in composing a photograph so there is no reason why this process should not be modified, sometimes to great creative effect, under the enlarger.

Following this line of thought I realised that there was no reason why I should not use multiple images if this was appropriate. This in turn made me think of the pictures I had taken of the young saplings in Blenheim Park with dramatic early morning skies in the background. Individually they had not satisfied me. However, by printing pairs of five separate images with different tonal values, I found I could suggest an avenue of young trees as night became day and we walked between them.

From then on I never worried if I found it difficult to select a single image. The day we attended an auction at Christie's is a case in point. The visual drama could not have been at a lower ebb. Nevertheless I went about my task and had soon exposed four rolls of film. Far from confident, we were just about to leave when I noticed a pair of hands a few feet away idly counting a wad of £50 notes as if it were Monopoly money. It was the best chance I had had so far.

Despite my excitement, when I saw the result I didn't feel that the image worked on its own. Instinct told me that it might if I repeated it three times on the same page. Quite why this is successful I still find hard to say. It may have something to do with the way people sometimes blink and take another look when they think their eyes are deceiving them. Whatever the reason, my pleasure at arriving at a solution was compounded when Stephen showed me his work. Quite by chance the shape of the words on the page mimicked exactly the triplicate nature of the image.

A coincidence like this had occurred once before. On reviewing work in progress we noticed that the shape of the verses in the 25 January, Waterloo poem was identical to the shape of the Jesus-like figure lying sprawled in front of the fire. Again there was this strange sense that the work itself had taken on a life independently of its creators!

Asked if I would supply some technical details I would instead prefer to record the overall approach I adopted rather than the detail as applied to each image. My reason for this is partly because my *modus operandi* does not include noting down F-stops, lenses and shutter speeds as I go but also because the darkroom often has as much to do with the final image as the individual settings on camera and lens.

Modern 35mm SLRs and film emulsions give great flexibility to the documentary photographer without an unacceptable loss of print quality. Most of the images in this book were taken on a Nikon FE2, a camera now no longer made but aimed originally as much at the amateur as the professional market. Two of the images, and I defy anyone to guess which, were taken with an Olympus XA compact! I also used a Nikon F3, a Nikon F4 for the Epilogue, and on one occasion a Fuji 645S professional. The lenses were high quality Nikkors with focal lengths ranging from 18mm to 105mm. One image was taken with a 200mm lens.

For purely subjective reasons I favoured Ilford FP4 when using a fine grain film (100 ASA) and Kodak Tri X (400 ASA) when shooting in less favourable lighting conditions. I also used the then recently launched Kodak TMAX 3200 film which allowed me to work without flash in very poor lighting conditions. Many professionals do not like TMAX and I share their reservations at the faster speeds. However, the contrast and grain it produces in very flat dull light was sometimes exactly what I was looking for.

Generally speaking 'art' photography belongs to the domain of the medium and large format camera. I hope this book demonstrates that this need not always be the case.

RICHARD MADDEN

THE POEMS

From the beginning I was concerned that the form of the poems should reflect the variety of experiences we were to cover. I was also anxious that the poetry should be accessible; sophistication is very different from complication. While Richard II sat in prison bemoaning his self-inflicted predicament, he cried: "I wasted time and now doth time waste me". There are few lines bigger, or simpler. It seems a fair enough precedent to trust.

Most of the poems were written within a week or two of the event we visited. This left little time for 'recollection in tranquillity'. Although the demand of the form was relentless, I found that its appetite was a healthy pressure and very much enjoyed the attempt to sate it. However, some of the experiences were harder to write about than others – particularly depressing if Richard had come up with an exciting image. And yet, as so often happens, the poems most fought for often turned out to be the ones of which I'm most proud.

Approaching publication the inevitable redrafting process has been difficult. It was obviously a sensitive area as I was anxious not to violate the spirit of the project. However, I decided that if a poem captured my experience of the time, then it should not be changed. But if I felt that the poem really didn't work, and was impeding access to the subject, I worked on it, or very occasionally replaced it with something entirely new.

And now the work is frozen by the process of publication. The meddling's over and I dare say in time some of it will beg for attention it will never get. And so I hope it will always be. For now the next poems are waiting. And they are making me curious.

STEPHEN CLARK

WILDLIFE

There are places where only
The spiders crawl, stringing
Webs between the bulrushes and
Hanging out the flies.
And on those lazy Sunday afternoons
When the larvae doze and the
Tadpoles settle down for tea,
The spiders scuttle out to see
How the wildlife is getting on . . .
The tin mines are still.
The young ones have moved on.
The lorries from the continent have grown.
The verges are grey.
The public house is quiet.
The old couple from 47
Watch the time of day.
And having despaired of
The tired flowers on the infant's grave
The spiders leg it home.
And the larvae stir.
And the tadpoles nod their welcome.
There are special times when to
Rest one's feet on several stools,
And to reach for a scandalous book
(*Fly Catcher* maybe)
Is the perfect end to a perfect day.
Time to reflect on the strange ways
Of the wildlife in their cottages:
For on a quiet day,
After the rain,
You can hear them reminisce.

A DERBYSHIRE VILLAGE
Autumn in Derbyshire has
grown thin and the tourists
have left.

NOTES OF SPIRITUAL REVELATION

Sitting, stiffly, in a suit.
Feeling persil white and not so innocent.
A long way from Handel.
Hallelujah!

A heathen held by dance and trance.
An agnostic accosted by open arms.
An atheist anaesthetised by smiles and charm.
A flurry of doubt nestles amid the self-consciousness.
I could be wrong.

Take it a little higher.

Between the periodic collections and the
Chastising of women for their cyclical blood,
I felt beauty.
No-one was more surprised.

Take it a little higher.

For these are only notes.
Notes for the people outside.
Notes for the strangers to strange faiths.
Notes for those who can only remain witnesses.
Notes for the ones who have stopped looking.

And still the incense burns.
And the music knocks and waits to be answered.
And the prayers of the players nag.
And the sweat of the trance drips down my retina
If I allow my eyes to rest.
So now I keep them open.
Awake.
I cannot say why.
Or for whom.
Or when, and if, they will close.
Or even who opened them.
For these are only notes for the cynic's smile.

*THE CELESTIAL
CHURCH OF CHRIST,
ISLINGTON*
*During the service
members of the
congregation sometimes go
into trance. While in this
state they deliver messages
for other members of the
church which are written
down as they speak. The
papers on which these
messages are written are
headed "Notes of
Spiritual Revelation".*

PRESENTS

Beneath his scrumpled rizla skin,
Behind the gums and growing nose,
I know there's always someone in.

What he does or where he goes
While caged by comfy chair and frame,
Is kept as close as embryos.

He hasn't always been the same.
He's living proof he's lived a life
But keeps me at my guessing game;

The rumours are, as always, rife.
But truths will always stay unwrapped
Without a patient paperknife.

Beneath his paper skin he's trapped:
Unlike the presents round the tree
He'll keep his secrets safe from me.

THE AVENUE

A queue of amputees awaits backstage,
Quiet now their hour of fretting's done;
A generation burned before old age
Bequeathing younger trees the winter sun.
Spotlit saplings revel in the glow
Of smiles of early ramblers like ourselves,
They do not know the grip of frost and snow
Or how their parents lie as books and shelves.
We watch them reach, we watch them take their time,
We'll tell our children's children how they grew,
For they will be the ones to swing and climb
The limbs that stretch and trace an avenue.
I hope they see between their falls and bumps
The lichen sleep on soft, forgotten stumps.

THE GROUNDS OF BLENHEIM PALACE, OXFORDSHIRE
In the grounds there used to be an avenue of elm trees a mile long. The trees all died with the rest of the country's elms. They were cut down, leaving only stumps. The avenue has recently been replanted with lime trees. They are only saplings, but the shape of the avenue is beginning to emerge again.

TAKING THE MICK

The rock is rolled
Just one more time
Before the crowd.

Shiny with a
Life-time of flash
Bulbs and stage lights;

Reflecting our
Pally smiles and
Bright with chatter;

Flirting fluent
French and clutching
The vodaphone;

Revelling in
The business of
Rhythm and Blues;

Juggling next day's
Copy with white
Light wit and sex.

And though we all
Pretend he just
Sings with a band,

And banter like we
Drink with him on
Saturday nights,

Deep down we know
We came to sit
On pews and pray:

Sweat, Jumpin' Jack;
Let us offer
Our candles high;

Make us Ruby
Tuesday on the
Last tube home.

FAME
At a press conference Mr
Jagger seemed in as fine
fettle as ever.

*SMITHFIELD MARKET
– 7.30 A.M.*
*Two vegetarians make an
early morning start.
Although animals are no
longer slaughtered on the
site, there is plenty to keep
the knees weak and the
stomach churning.*

END

In the twinkling of a dead eye
I wait for the wink. The nod.
In the festival of omnivores,
Where the slap of meat on slab
Is dull and ordinary, I have a
Ring side seat. But no applause.

And the blood is never thick.
It runs thin and lost. We are
Warned against slipping on stone,
For the grease of trodden fat is left
To be sluiced when the work is done.
When the flesh has left the bone.

The casual precision of each stroke
Of the blade is compulsive. Watch.
The corpses part with ease.
Somewhere I expected resistance,
A tricky tendon, a clinging muscle.
I didn't know bodies slice like cheese.

Does mine? Maybe if I lean a
Little closer, while the man in
Stained whites chats to his friend,
I can meet the axe before it falls,
Wince, and drip upon the iron hook.
Another early morning end.

PENANCE

There's nothing like a real fire to come home to.
Can't beat it.
You ask 'em.
It's true.

Singing through the toxic fumes of plastic crates and foam.
"Wherever I lay
My hat, that's
My home".

Underneath the arches. Winter night. Waterloo.
Watching in the
Shadows as they
Watch you.

And the chocolate's passed around with the can of Special Brew.
Tastes real good
When there's sod
All else to do.

And Carl with his dog, Penance, finds one more song.
And it won't be so
Bad when the nights
Aren't so long.

So that's alright then. No need to get annoyed.
They do no harm
And they're easy
To avoid.

And the man with the empty eyes who sleeps among the ash,
With nothing in his
Pocket but other
People's cash,

Looks as though he's found himself his very own pyre;
Where else do you go
When your home
Is fire?

*WATERLOO, BENEATH
THE ARCHES – 2 A.M.*
*As the makeshift fire dies
down, songs are sung and
beer is sipped before the
lucky ones like Carl and his
dog, Penance, move on to
the shelters. Only a few
remain.*

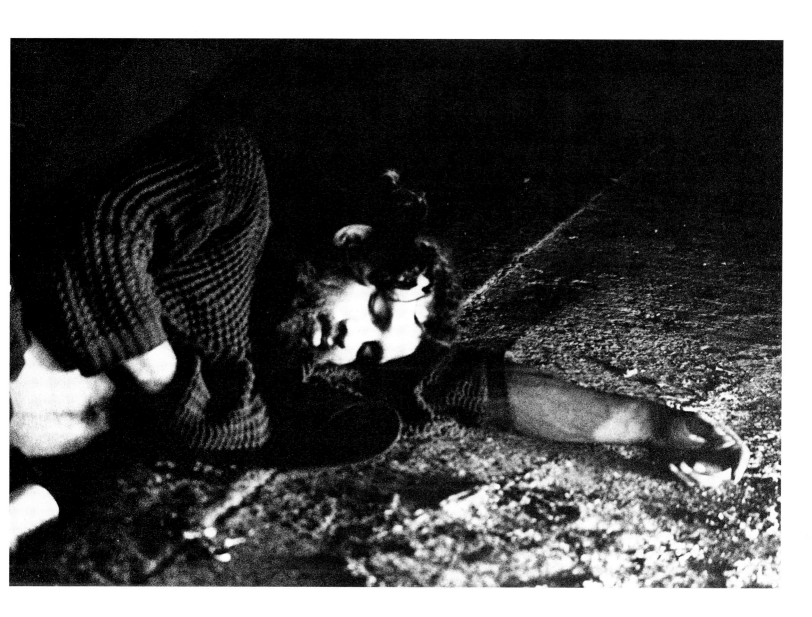

NO ONE LIKES US

AT "THE DEN" – HOME OF MILLWALL FC
This poem, like the anthem of Millwall's supporters, "No One Likes Us", should be sung to the tune of "Sailing" by Rod Stewart.

We have waited, with breath baited,
For the weekend, when they play.
'Cos we love Millwall
And we love football
But you know fuck all
So stay away.

Get some 4X, straight down our necks,
Then to welcome, Liverpool.
Watch the coppers
Try to stop us
But they'll come croppers,
We're so cool.

Here's the Big Match, there's just one catch,
Same old story, lost again.
A Sunday passes,
No catharsis,
We'll break their arses
'Cos we're such men.

If you hear their cries, we apologise,
Just a Stanley blade, in the chest.
With all that boozin'
Who likes loosin'
It ain't amusin'
Fuck the rest.

If you think we came, just to watch the game,
Then you've got it wrong, that's just hype.
We're here to be true Brit,
To dole out the shit,
To make sure we fit
The archetype.

You see on mass, we're all working class,
Or as Saatchi says, C2DE.
But we don't give a toss,
You see it's your loss,
If you call us dross
That's how we'll be.

'Cos no-one likes us, no-one likes us,
No-one likes us, we don't care.
We are Millwall,
Super Millwall,
We are Millwall,
From the Den.

REFLECTIONS
*A grim Friday in February
at the end of the decade. It
seems as good a time as any
to reflect on what the
eighties were all about.*

SIGNS OF THE TIME

(Three Haikus for Maggie)

The Nanny with the
Medicine, humourless and
Dour, is in her prime.

The veneer's getting
Thinner; the chaps with all the
Power learn to mime.

While the pigeons perched
On Eros watch us dance in
Coca-Cola time.

SIZEWELL NUCLEAR
REACTOR
There are no sci-fi domes,
Pompidou Centre
outlines or faded CND
banners. Instead there are
people, with their dogs,
strolling by of a Sunday
afternoon.

TOMORROW ALWAYS COMES

A walk along the open beach
Of a seaside afternoon;
We'd play beside a winter tide
Caught 'twixt sun and moon.
We'd watch our children play
Between the drift wood and the dune;
Remember when a Sunday dusk
Would always come too soon . . .

We'd listen to the wind and waves,
To the secrets of the sea,
To the gentle hum from concrete walls
Where the beach huts used to be.
We'd hang our socks on barbed wire fence
And paddle after tea,
For the water was always warmest
By our seaside factory.

And remember how our children grew,
Nurtured by the sun,
We sacrificed too much perhaps,
But in the end we won.
For they'll pass on our Sundays
To their daughter, to their son:
The gifts we give our little ones
Cannot be undone.

EMPTY

the meeting ends.
the room vacuates
its sub committee.
the minutes are
emptied into the
Apple Mac.

redundant, the short
handed copy is harlem
globe trotted into the
basket.

and the wind searches
for the basket-balls of short hand,
turning over old leaves
and chuckling at Any Other Business.

and at the end of the day
when all's said and done
and it's over bar the shouting
the waste paper basket is emptied.

empty.

into dustbins which are emptied.

and the little hollow
(in the middle of the dump
between the coke cans
and inner tubes)
waits patiently to be

into dustcarts which are emptied.

filled by tomorrow's meeting,
when item three on the agendum

onto wasteland which is full.

will be presented by a
man who empties his
pores in a marble room.

the wind has no idea
what pleasures lie ahead:
the memos to the moribund
while we practise being dead.

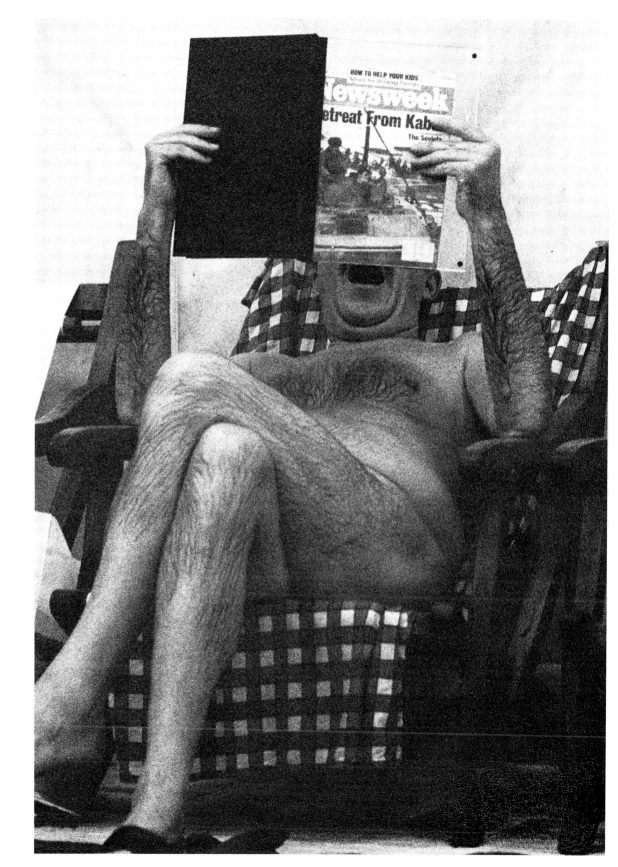

THE TURKISH BATH AT THE RAC CLUB, PICCADILLY

The steam rooms are full of 'the people at the top' cleansing themselves of the dirt of the day.

ANONYMITY
"I don't mind if my skull ends up on a shelf, as long as it's got my name on it" – Debbie Harry.

ANON

For unknown soldiers
Beneath their slabs,
For still-born lives
In unnamed graves,
For the poets who left us
Unclaimed words,
For the severed roots
Of wives and slaves.

For the man in the fire
With one gold tooth,
For the child on the telly
Who's hollow and old,
For the girls who leave bundles
On hospital steps,
For the Maya whose stories
Can never be told.

For the husk of the Beaker Man,
Naked and shy,
For the widow of war,
Gang-raped at dawn,
For the rebel who fights
With a cross in a box,
For the child-abused parents
Whose children are torn.

Sing.

Sally, tongue curled carefully on her upperlip, gently stroked a coat of colour on the tissue-paper. At last the balsa wood skeleton disappeared from sight and Sally smiled as the garage filled with the sharp fumes of yellow gloss paint. Soon the fuselage would be finished and the wings, which had been ready for weeks, could be nestled into place.

Sally always made the wings first. It was the wings that she loved; the wings that made the impossible possible; the subtly shaped simplicity of a wingspan that carried weights too heavy to drift alone; wings that broke all the rules (later Sally would learn that of course they merely followed rules and were governed by predictable laws. As with most answers she was to find this interesting, but disappointing).

The next morning Sally got up early and climbed into her best dungarees. The weather was perfect. A slight wind, a clear sky and a warm sun. She ran to the barn and checked the paint-work from the night before. The surface was now taut and shiny and Sally enjoyed the smooth of the finish as she gently lowered the wings into place. Then she made sure that the little door still opened. The door had been hard to make as it wasn't in the original plans. But she wanted a door that opened and closed like doors should, and was worried that the final coat of paint might have glued it up. But it swung easily on its tiny hinges and Sally smiled in relief and pleasure. It's the details that count, she thought to herself.

Then she checked that the wheels turned easily and that the propeller spun silently against its washer. The propeller had been the hardest part to make. It had taken three attempts to get it perfect. The drawings on the plan, a series of figure of

GOING AWAY
For the next five weeks we are boarding aeroplanes and working abroad. The themes and dates for the photopoems have been prearranged so that, although apart, the work can continue.

eights from different angles, were very confusing and in the end it had taken some help from mum to interpret the cross-sections and elevations.

Sally was very impressed. She noted to herself that mums seem to be very good at these things when there isn't a daddy around. Although she still missed daddy. A lot. She understood why he'd gone to live in America, and she even liked the new mum he'd found, but only seeing him once a year, at Christmas, never seemed enough. By the time the presents were unwrapped it was time to come home again. And there were times she just couldn't wait. Why don't grown-ups understand just how long it is till Christmas?

Anyway, Sally was very proud of the propeller. Anyone can stick a ready made propeller on a plane. It takes skill and patience to make your own.

Once Sally was in the field the wind seemed a little stronger than she'd thought. She threw a blade of grass above her head and watched as it fell a few feet to her right. But today was the day and Sally knew that it was simply a matter of adjusting the weights and trimming the ailerons. Then came the winding of the propeller. This would be the first time that the structure had to take any strain. This was why everything had to be done so carefully; every join, every drop of glue, every tiny pin had to be perfect or the strain of the twisting length of rubber that ran the length of the fuselage would be too much.

As she turned the carefully sculptured figure of eight she listened to the balsa tightening. More and more she turned until she felt the band itself would take no more. Then, keeping hold of one of the propeller's blades, she placed the aeroplane on the ground and wedged a chip of wood between the centre of the propeller and its washer to stop it from

spinning. Sally looked around. The house was still quiet. Mum often slept in on Sundays and except for the soft chatter of the stream that ran through the orchard, there was nothing to intrude. Almost nothing to say goodbye to. So she didn't. And mum would understand. She understood everything.

The church bells were just striking ten as Sally cautiously opened the door of the plane and climbed in. She settled into place, carefully spreading her weight so as not to put too much strain on the frame, and then looked around one last time. She was very pleased with the windows. Not a fingerprint in sight. And not even the cows had looked up. Then she opened the front window and tugged gently at the chip of wood that was jamming the propeller. The sudden noise was deafening as the spinning band unravelled and the surge of the plane, as it leapt forward on its easily turning wheels, threw Sally back into place.

And then the wheels were off the ground and she could hardly breathe with excitement. She was flying! She was flying! She was going to see daddy and it wasn't even Christmas! Sally laughed as she watched the world disappear through the blur of the propeller blades. This was the best present he'd ever given her. And mum will understand, she thought. She understands everything . . .

STRANGE

            Through
        their
                    eyes
                        it
        didn't
                    seem
            surreal.

In fact it seemed perfectly ordinary.

(When I was young it was hard:
There were no grasshoppers in our yard.
And though I was fond
Of our garden pond,
You try
Being knee high
To a fish.)

And in the short journey from the palette to the page,
I watched the children climb inside a different-seeing age.

                    The
        people
            having
                    paid,
        watched
            them
                draw
                    and
            stayed
        longer
                    than
    Miro
            could
                    have
        dared
                to
            hope.

For while silos wait with goods unhurled
Two little girls gave birth to the world.

CHILDREN – NEPAL AND NEW YORK
In Nepal a child meets a camera.

In the Surrealist room, in the Museum of Modern Art, Manhattan, two young children, Anika and Lisa, copy a painting into their drawing books. The painting is The Birth of the World *by Joan Miro.*

THURSDAY **16 MARCH**

AMERICANS – ITALY
AND NEW YORK
In Rome, a group of young
Americans enjoy the sights.

In Manhattan, the
Americans enjoy each
other.

CRAZINESS

I want
to come
back.

The
openness
grips.

Craziness
is friendlier

than stiffened
upper lips.

Dear Della,

Flight fine. Cheap wine. Can't sleep.
Snow's deep. New York's long walks,
full bars, cheap cars, street lights,
scared nights. I fear stay here too
short. Have caught • Can't face slow
pace back home" syndrome. True
joke: saw bloke on street, bare feet,
with cup, fed up, half dead, cup
read • I ♥ NY" no doubt held out for
dimes.... Strange times.
    Love you. Guess who...

AWAY FROM HOME – BELIZE AND NEW YORK
Life on Ambergris Cay is a picture postcard.
The streets of Manhattan are bleak, cold and crammed with choice.
Photograph by Richard Madden

POSTCODE

word

DIMES

The busker hollers
Unaware of John
Who'd love to throw dimes.

Hold on.

I listen to him.
The answer isn't
Blowing in the wind.

Hold on.

And during the third
Minute I forget
Why I am silent.

Hold on.

And when the silence
Ends the busker stops
To gather his dimes.

Hold on.

When someone needs a
Brownie point they'll set
You free. Set you free.

Hold on.

I hope you fill a
Thousand hats with dimes
Before you die again.

Hold on.
Hold on.
Hold on.

*THREE MINUTES FOR
JOHN McCARTHY –
BELIZE AND NEW YORK
It is three years since John
McCarthy was kidnapped in
Beirut. Today his girlfriend
and supporters ask just three
minutes of our time to think
of John.*

THE ENVIRONMENT –
BELIZE AND NEW YORK
While the rainforests burn, a
gentleman with a large fragrant
cigarette asks, "Where is the
world?"

WHERE?

There is no wilderness;
no nothingness to hem

us in and keep us out;
nothing virgin; nowhere

untouched by the fruit of
ingenious tests, dusting

the planet with a light
coating of silent death;

no hill or stream or tree
unturned, unchained, uncut.

A LAZY DAY – GUATEMALA
AND NEW YORK
Some days are for wasting …

LAZY DAY

The bird that sits
(wrapped in wings and
on my window sill)
Quietly asks
What shape the day will be.

I do not want to answer.
Today is tired.
It has run out of cookies
And its ashtray is full.

I exercise my right
As a free member of
A democratic society,
To discover the most comfortable position in which to lie in bed:
It takes all day to confirm I made the right decision 28 years ago.
But it's always best to know.
For sure.

At least I now
Have something to say
To my feathery friend.

She blinks,
Unconcerned,
And starts her journey home.
Fuck.
Why should her beginning
Be my end?

THE BELGRANO
Seven years ago today, the death of 368 Argentinians was greeted with the headline "GOTCHA!" by The Sun. *The battle between the realities of war and the jingoistic coverage of some of the media had begun.*

GOTCHA!

We etch our boundaries
In seas and rock and snow.
Empires. Countries. Backyards.
We stake our passing claims
Crudely, pissing on our
Carefully carved lampposts.

And we kill. And we die.
Impatient, proud to exclude,
We drive shards of metal
Into each other's bodies
And pile ourselves high.
It is a willing pyre.

Without love, without taste,
Sick with the need to prove,
Trapped within blood drawn lines,
We hack away at our
Selves, never learning that,
Unwhole, we bleed to death.

HAL-AN-TOW

There was the carefully lying down
In clean cotton as
The sunburn scraped on the sheets,
Tired with the effort of too
Many words and the pain of laughter.

There was the waking up and checking
The red had softened to brown
Before climbing down to the damp beach
To watch a naked child running
To cuddle the waves.

There was the listening to stories
Of fishermen; of rocks and wrecks
And brown-and-white photographs.

There was the watching of a disappearing
Moon that slithered away, slice by slice
With each dusk.

There was a Flora day.
While the trombones blew
And the gentry danced
And the children skipped
And the young men and women
Swung ever closer,
There was the losing of time;
The climbing inside of stories
And photographs
And dusks
And child's arms.

And when at last the town
Slipped into the present,
We lay warmed and silent
Between the cotton,
Listening to the waves.

CORNWALL
The day after Flora
Day, Helston's ancient
spring festival, was
spent on beaches
watching the sun rise
and the night fall.

SAGA

A quiet duet of smiles in Regent's Park,
A game that only lovers could have played,
Knowing all the time the sun will fade
And leave them to the joys of after-dark.
For just before the light completes its arc,
Before they find their whispers in the shade,
No amount of dew could so persuade
The fire not to kindle from the spark.
For summer love is sweating in their palms
And shining from the smugness of their grins;
Just take it from this jaded raconteur
Their flush of hope was not without its charms.
The dusk is close and so the tale begins:
The saga of their private *pas de deux*.

REGENT'S PARK

A beautiful spring day. An afternoon of swans, grassy slopes, and lovers between rose beds …

GREENFINGER

Down in the jungle where Greenfinger lives
The judge has awarded first prize,
To the bonsai and cacti, those strange artifacti,
Each one a plant in disguise.

Greenfinger lurks with her friends in the tent
Sniffing and rolling her eyes,
"It's such a good looker – the poise of that Yucca!"
She nods with the grace of the wise.

Now Greenfinger sits by the topiary display,
I can still hear her friends eulogize,
She'll often relive it, the sight of that privet,
Of entropy cut down to size.

Five o'clock strikes and the scrummage begins,
They'll murder to get the best buys,
O where was Our Saviour, for Greenfinger's behaviour
Would've caught Millwall fans by surprise.

Greenfinger's on tip-toe, she's climbing the trellis,
"Gimme roses, yes roses!" she cries,
She's flailing at strangers with wilting hydrangeas
In a manner she'd usually despise.

Till bearing her booty in evergreen hands
In a way her excitement belies,
She strides through the crushes of bulbs and bulrushes
To return to her lair in Belsize.

But after the show when the stands are all bare
And Greenfinger's left with her prize,
She sits by herself and stares at the shelf:
At the vase where her one red rose dies.

THE CHELSEA FLOWER SHOW

On the last day of the Chelsea Flower Show at 5 p.m. precisely a bell is rung and the exhibits become available for sale; a chance for everybody to own the very best that the experts have to offer.

I

A golden day, I wandered by the stream
  And saw a crowd of strangers on the bank,
Strange indeed for seemed almost a dream
  For whom I have my tainted nights to thank.
But though my thoughts were such that some may deem
  Unworthy, of a mind both dark and dank,
I swear I saw a crowd of chinless folk
Who though absurd with ringing tones they spoke.

II

And so I chose a grassy spot to lie
  Amongst the ferns and sheltered by the trees,
I watched the speckled thrush and hunted fly
  Then traced the tireless journeys of the bees
And waited for the hour the boats come by,
  To see them cut the ripples and the breeze.
Just as patience will with time desires sate
I waited for the honoured oars of eight.

III

At last in sight, those youths bedecked in flowe
  Pulling 'gainst the current 'fore the crowd,
Who can surmise the long and lonely hours
  They strove to make their portly parents prou
Behold the young ones revel in their powers,
  And proudly claim their privilege aloud;
For upright in their boats by thousands seen
They doff their hats to Windsor, Eton, Queen.

ETON –
"FOURTH OF JUNE"
Eton's open day has as its
centrepiece a procession of
boats. Successive teams of
schoolchildren row past a
vast gathering of parents.
While still moving they
stand precariously in their
boats and doff their hats to
Eton, Windsor and, of
course, the Queen. This
poem is dedicated to the
least likely of old Etonians:
Percy Bysshe Shelley.

IV

But though these be the masters of the morrow
  They too are plagued by twists of cruel fate,
Though silver coins can time and fortune borrow
  There are those Gods no guilders can placate.
And thus I watch without a hint of sorrow
  An incident with pleasure I narrate:
One young man whilst witnessed by the horde
Salutes the Queen and then falls overboard.

V

Methinks I see the swans and moorhens smile,
  Methinks I feel the sun glow ever warm;
A thousand stiffened lips grow soft awhile
  And watch a dripping youth ride out the storm.
But when at last they're tired of the trial
  Then cheerful through the village they will swarm,
Where the champagne and the glory overflows;
Where the barmaid vows, "One day we'll come to blows".

*OUTSIDE THE CHINESE
EMBASSY*
*On the night of the massacre in
Tiananmen Square, Beijing, a
group of Chinese students gather
outside the Chinese Embassy in
London.*

FIRST FEAR

the news is drip-fed.
Chinese whispers,
quiet with disbelief and
warmed only by candlelight,
drift with the incense.

only numbers count;
round numbers.

and here,
where a cross-court volley is "extraordinary",
we are left silent.

blanched bodies around another square,
so that someday
somebody can
abstain.

THE MISSIONARY POSITION

I have a right.
God given, power driven.
You will listen.

I know The Truth.
Undeterred I'll spread the word.
No boundaries.

Have no fear.
From Holy scribe to African tribe.
I understand.

Surrender.
You cannot fight such blinding light.
There is one way.

Mine.

BILLY GRAHAM AT
UPTON PARK
At the end of the sermon
members of the
congregation are asked to
come forward and commit
themselves to Christ.
They are greeted by
"counsellors" eager to
reply to every question,
deal with every problem,
write down every address.
The following
conversation was
overheard between the
lady in the wheelchair
and the bright young
counsellor:

LADY:
I feel I can't go to church
because I haven't been
forgiven all my sins.

COUNSELLOR:
I here, now, forgive you
all your sins.

LADY:
If I've been forgiven, why
can't I walk?

COUNSELLOR:
Maybe God has decided
you should be patient….

MIDSUMMER DAY
IN OXFORD
A large garden party at
Magdalen College in
honour of the Queen of
Spain and Andrei
Sakharov.

STRANGER

Time has leaked.
A tiny droplet of an era
Has dripped into today.

For once I am the stranger.
Soon they will start shouting
So that I may understand.

I want to tell them about
Deep Pan Pizzas and
The Chaos Theory and
Michael Jackson,
But I don't.

I stand mute.
Deafened by mores
And blinded by nuance.

CELLS

The film of dust that settles
Damply on the shine of the tracks
When the rush hour has rushed
Is a mist of dead cells;
The flakelets of old skin brushed
Off by cuffs and collars.

We are crumbling at the edges,
Followed by that scaly haze
Inhaled by strangers unaware
That they too are being breathed
In and out on tainted air
While waiting for the trains.

It is not something we can leave to
Another time. For even when we wish
Fresh air and scamper to the beach,
The scour of the on-shore breeze erodes
Whatever's in its reach,
Scraping at the face of the cliff.

IF YOU KNEW . . .

If you knew
That I lie in
My sheets and
Turn us over
In my mind,
And see us
Locked in each
Other's bodies
And remember my
Love knocking
At your womb;
And that I
Pause on the
Slopes of your
Breasts and smile
As I recall the
Tickle of your
Nipples on my
Tongue; that I
Wrap my hand
Around the
Hardness of my
Need for you,
That I close my
Eyes to closer
Feel the smooth
Of your skin, the
Course of hair, the
Moist of your lips;
If you knew that I
Stain my sheets with
My memories of you,
Re-running every
Tease, every suck,
Every thrust, every
Swallow; and that
Sated I roll over
And fall asleep to
The smell of you
On my pillow;
Would you wish to
Snatch my memories
Like the letters
And the photographs
You burnt?

For when I please
Myself alone,
Your past lies bare
For me to own.

MASTURBATION
Lying in bed, trying to plan the next day, my mind drifted, as it often does, to past lovers and the love we made.

TWENTY YEARS ON

When it got too late for my eyes I would be wrapped up and carried upstairs to bed. Along with the biscuits and glass of sherry I'd wait in silence for the footfalls of our annual imposter. Mummy told me it didn't matter that we only had central heating . . . that he would get in somehow. He must have known when sleep stole my curiosity for I never saw him fill my stocking. I never saw him at all.

> I dreamed of sellotape and marzipan
> And the note I'd sent the presents-man.

And one year, beneath the drying needles and tinsel, lay a parcel wrapped in gold. We sat in a circle and took turns to tussle with the sticky tape and string. I left my golden gift to last and when at last it was revealed . . . Nobody had ever seen such a beautiful train. Red and blue with wheels that turned. All day I drove that train through wild frontiers . . . and after tea and mince pies I travelled into space.

> Twenty years on I saw what richer men do;
> Twenty-seven thousand on a tin choo choo.

I was impressed. It can't be easy to look authoritative when bidding for a toy train. Of course I'm not saying that some didn't twitch a little when a particularly shiny model came into view. Some even rang in and had offers made on their behalf. I couldn't help thinking it would have been cheaper to write to the presents-man. And I wondered, when they got home and unwrapped their prize, where were they going to travel?

MAIDA VALE BABY

Sleep well my sweet.
Barney Bunny in the bedroom
Is not afraid.
He misses not the warren
Where all his mates were made.

Dream safe my love.
You can trust your Wally Whale
Beside the bed.
He too knows not when strangers
Turn the sea to red.

Don't cry my child.
Leo Lion and Henrietta Hen
Have no tales.
For round you in the cot they lie
Where innocence prevails.

Smile on my babe.
The bearded faces mean no harm
Despite their breath.
Allow them just this once to think
Of birth instead of death.

Forgive them, love.
Outlive them and the false-teeth smiles
They wear to shape their lips.
They did not choose their weathered scars
And calloused fingertips.

BABIES
Oliver and friends.

Understand my sweet.
Someone crept into their heads
And took away their toys.
They frown because they can't recall
The joy of being boys.

STEPS

The tree will wrap one
Ring around itself
Before September.

The rust will bite deep
Beneath the shine of
The cold iron rails.

The poster will roar
The same absurd lies
In the same type-face.

The street-lamp's red glow
Will tell kids when to
Go to bed and dream.

The bricks will dandruff
Powder in the heat
And flakes in the snow.

The blithe couple will
Grow old behind their
Sightless city eyes.

And the boy, and those
Who sit on steps, will
Sit and wait on steps.

ON THE STREETS
*You don't have to look very
far to find someone who has
stopped looking.*

AFRIKA

It is strange to think
(On the thirty eight
to Cambridge Circus)
that the lady with
the blue rinse came from
Afrika.

That the fair haired gent
who cannot keep his
eyes to himself, who
cannot stop licking
his thin lips, came from
Afrika.

That the new baby
opposite who's as
bright as her blanket,
and boasts a Jewish
nose (already), came from
Afrika.

But they did. So long
ago they do not
remember shedding
their skins. I watch them
scuttle, like hermit
crabs between shells: pink,
raw and vulnerable.

A MEMORIAL, HIGHBURY
CORNER, LONDON
In the middle of the borough of
Islington, renowned for its left-
wing stance, a memorial to the
soldiers who fought in the Boer
War takes pride of place at the
corner of Highbury Fields.

"HOW SLEEP THE BRAVE WHO SINK TO REST,
BY ALL THEIR COUNTRY'S WISHES BLESS'D."

————

IN HONOUR OF
NINETY-EIGHT ISLINGTONIANS
WHO DIED FOR THEIR COUNTRY
IN THE SOUTH AFRICAN WAR,
1899-1903.

————

ERECTED BY THEIR FELLOW-TOWNSMEN
JULY, 1905.

————

WAVES

A SUNNY DAY IN BRIGHTON
Oh, I do like to be beside the seaside.

Waiting on the lip of the land
I watch the waves
Stumble on the beach.
Stretched too thin they reach
With white-tipped cold and bubbled hand
Then seep between the
Rattle of the stones.

They have travelled many miles to die
Upon these slopes.
And the sea that pumps
In my veins rushes
At the sound of their deaths,
Their splendid deaths,
While the herring gulls keen.

But once these deaths gave birth;
Their last breaths
Breathing life into land.
And so we crawl,
Always crawling,
Back to the sea. To feel what our
Beginnings felt.

But we are restless. We spin
On piers and drown
The sea in summer screams.
In packed-lunch tribes
We shimmy at the edge of the world;
Then wait for the snaps
To prove we were there.

INTO THE MIDDLE DISTANCE

The beginning of autumn strokes our cheeks.
While it is still warm, our eyes fix.
There is nothing to say. Nothing.
We have learnt to stare.

There is nothing idle about our curiosity.
How else do we make it a part of our lives?
What else can we do but adjust?
Slowly. In our own time.

The bouquets and silence are not for the dead.
They are for us.
What we have lost is important only
Because we remain.

So, left behind,
We blink. Lost.
After all,
We are still staring at Pompeii.

THE MARCHIONESS

The Herald of Free Enterprise. The Clapham Trains. Lockerbie. Hillsborough. Kings Cross Tube. Heisel Stadium. The Marchioness.

BEACH BUM PARTY AT A GAY PUB
Sue Pollard presides over a competition to judge the best dressed 'beach bum'. The tabloids would have loved it....

HEAVEN

His name was Phillipe.
I was seventeen
And Phillipe was French.
And that's how he kissed.

After closing time,
In the trembling glare
Of a frank street lamp,
We were both as hard

As the gravestone that
Bit into my spine.
And we came. And went.
And it was heaven.

And the girlfriend that
Laughs and doesn't mind
The scars on my back
Can have all of me.

SHOCKED

In down town LONDON yesterday, an evening of VICE was uncovered by two of our reporters. Witnesses said that people, ALL MEN, were seen DRINKING and DANCING until the small hours of the morning. The so called PARTY took place in a PUBLIC HOUSE. All of these MEN were BORN many years ago and yet all seemed to be having a very GOOD TIME.

By Stephen Clark

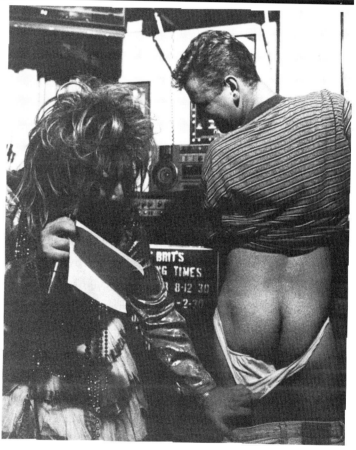

SCANTILY CLAD

"Yea, sometimes we come here dressed in beachwear", one of THEM admitted. After much research one of our reporters discovered that not half a mile away from the scene of last night's PARTY is a JUNIOR school that is used by many CHILDREN during the day. When asked about this, one of the MEN, dressed only in a T-SHIRT and SHORTS said, "Yea, I used to go there".

SEX

One of the party goers claimed to be a GREEN GROCER during the day as well as being a member of the local neighbourhood watch scheme. This is what our INNER CITIES are coming to! There were even rumours that one of the PARTICI-PANTS was a JUDGE who enjoyed socialising and play-ing SCRABBLE! Indeed it has been suggested that in his YOUNGER days he INDULGED in many word games such as crosswords and hangman.

SOCIALISTS

Although no scuba diving EQUIPMENT was found on the premises, it is suspected that many had used such DEVICES while on holiday. "Yea, it's easy stuff to get hold of if you know where to look", one of the MEN told us. "It's not that expensive and is a real THRILL to use." We can now reveal that one of them even went to EVENING CLASSES, sub-sidised by the local COUN-CIL, to learn about Marine Wildlife.

OZONE LAYER

According to one of our reporters on the scene the bar itself was littered with bowls of CRISPS and PEANUTS, many of which were being EATEN. Furthermore, later on in the NIGHT, large plates of SANDWICHES and cheese and onion QUICHES were passed around the public house for everyone to SHARE. "It was quite UNBELIEVABLE", said our reporter. "There were people reaching over one another to reach the food. There seemed to be HANDS everywhere you looked. And THEY were then EATING right in front of one another and yet every-one just turned a blind eye and carried on DANCING as if nothing was happening!"

GAY

One man admitted that he was even planning to go to church the following Sunday.

BOTTOM

Once the PROCEEDINGS were underway a very well known celebrity interviewed the COMPETITORS in the beachwear competition. We heard that their INTERESTS ranged from SWIMMING to GARDENING. On top of this we learnt that Phil from Hackney liked sunbathing with his FRIEND on regular SUMMER holidays. Then suddenly, to the DELIGHT of the crowd, one of the con-testants BARED his BOT-TOM. We at the DAILY MALE condemn outright this kind of wanton corrupt-ing behaviour regardless of how smooth, firm and entic-ing his BUTTOCKS might have been.

APPEAL

If we are to ever STAMP out this kind of public outrage it is essential that members of the public keep us fully up to date with where and when these sort of events are hap-pening. Ring us any time.

STOP PRESS

We have just heard that next week THEY are planning to hold a BARBECUE in the OPEN AIR and that both of our reporters have been invited.

BORED GAMES

If we all remember a day
So differently that it can only
Ever be a sum of our disparate
Interpretations;
If there is no
Absolute truth;
If we cannot be sure
That anything ever happens;
If we cannot know
That we are no more
Than figments of
One another's imaginations;
If we do exist but only
In order to replicate
A strip of DNA;
If life only means anything
Because we die;
If death only means anything
Because we live;
If we are born as nothing,
Die into nothing,
And merely breathe inbetween;
If I am a complex chemical soup,
A serendipitous meeting of matters,
And that is all;
Then why am I going
(dazed and dulled)
On a train and a bus
To do something
I don't want to do
For someone
I don't want to know;
And all to get some
Coloured notes
Whenever I pass "Go"?

Why?

GOING TO WORK
There are weekends of
friends and football,
relatives and roast dinners,
lounging about and love
making. Then there are
Monday mornings . . .

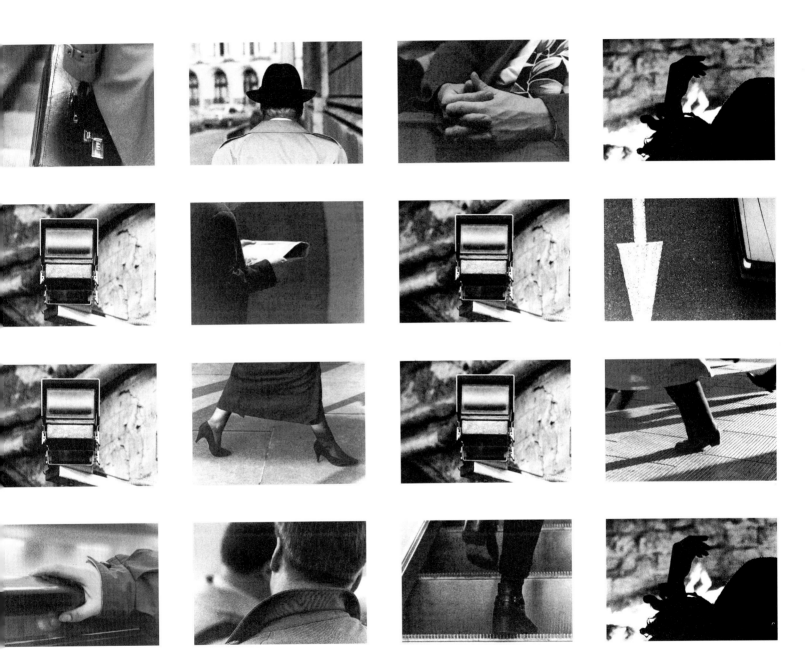

WORLDS APART

Different worlds
That rise and fall
On each other's horizons,
Peering distantly
At each other's light,
And moving ever further
From each other's heat.

It is an orbit
With direction
And no purpose.

It is two centres
Too lost in the blur
Of their own gaze.

If we are so blinded by our own light
That we cannot see the other stars,
How can we remind ourselves of how small we are?

And how bright we could be?

AGEING
In Tower Hamlets, London,
a class of ten year olds visit
their local residential home
for elderly people. It is a part
of the work of Magic Me, an
organisation that brings
children and old people
together on a weekly basis to
the benefit and amusement
of young and old.

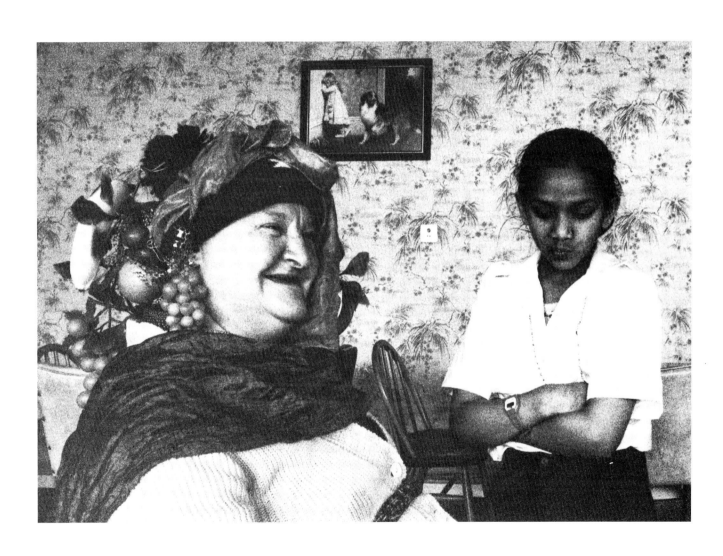

AIDS
Perhaps the most frightening aspect of the development of Aids is the growing awareness that we are only witnessing its early days. The threat is still in its infancy.

REMEMBERING

A too clever disease
Spreads name by name,
Hiding behind labels,
Nurtured by shame.

A savage sculptor chips
At lives; its tool
The oldest adage: it
Divides to rule.

Like us, it does not care
How it survives;
Like us, its blinkered greed
Destroys and thrives.

We have much in common,
We know its thirst;
And still we do not know
Who will die first.

But if we turn our backs,
Forget the dead,
We help the list of names
Quietly spread.

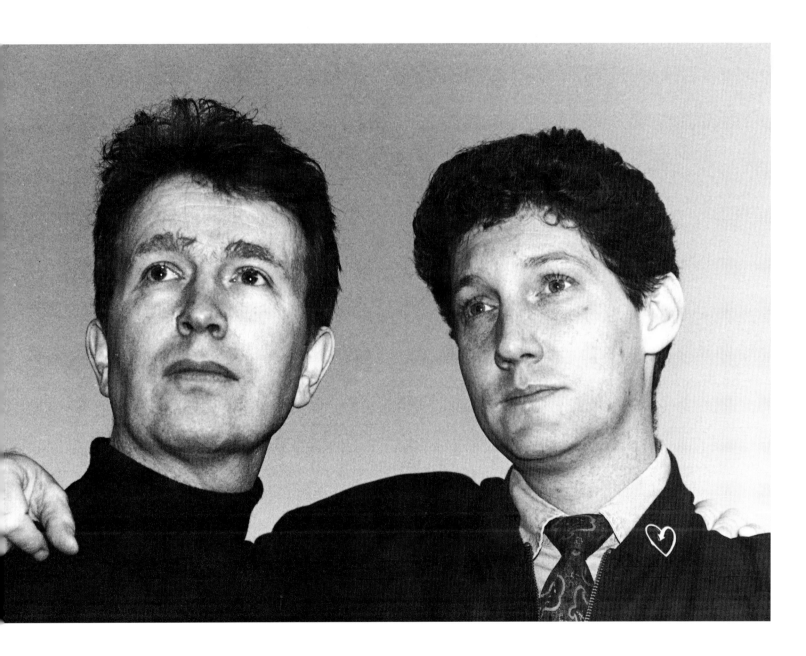

SATURDAY **30 SEPTEMBER**

*LANNER VEAN FARM,
CORNWALL*
*Some subjects will not be
ignored …*

LOVE

The first kiss was of ashtrays,
Of a nicotine laden tongue,
Of too much coke and brandy
At parties you have when young.

The second was like summer,
As gentle as sleeping breath,
As sweet as a child in mother's arms
Before it dreams of death.

The third was full of passion,
And tasted of lover's need,
Driven by fear that spells would break
My kisses turned to greed.

And now the world's become our shell,
We hear no other's call,
We've learnt that love can sit as still
As a cat on an autumn wall.

STONES

they are not
silent stones,
they speak as loud as
hills and bones.

they are shards
of another place,
each bleak and beaten
lichen-face

is proud with time;
in the circle of stone
the sweat hewn slabs
wait together and alone

while we fuss
and watch our backs
and rattle round
myopic tracks.

between the stones
i realize
where mystery is
the meaning lies.

STANDING STONES
Whether it be the Lochbuie
Stones, Tobermory or a
Dreamstone in the Avebury
Henge, they all have their
stories to tell.

SIGN OF THE TIMES

Docklands is the most potent
and appalling symbol of the
Thatcherite era. It is a
development that is motivated
purely by greed and leaves no
room for people, their real
needs and their relationships.
We live in a country where
success is measured not by the
coherence of the community
but by the popularity of the
advertising campaign.

THE POET ACCEPTS
NO RESPONSIBILITY FOR THE FORM
OR UNSUBTLETY OF, OR REFERENCE TO,
POLITICS APPEARING OR STAYING
(IN THIS POEM) (WHOSOEVER
WROTE IT) WHICH ARE AT THE
SOLE RISK OF THE PHOTOGRAPHER.

THE COMPANY ACCEPTS
NO RESPONSIBILITY FOR LOSS
OR THEFT OF, OR DAMAGE TO,
VEHICLES ENTERING OR PARKED
(IN THIS AREA) (HOWSOEVER
ARISING) WHICH ARE AT THE
SOLE RISK OF THE OWNERS.

WEDDING
"Don Mathew and Annie Mueller request the pleasure of the company of Stephen Clark and Richard Madden for the Blessing Service celebrating their marriage at St. Margaret's Church, Lowestoft."

A HAIKU FOR ANNIE

In grey rain a bride
in white plants green leaves between
the mottled gravestones.

GAME

Once upon an ancient world,
A brutal, feudal globe,
Only Bishops spoke to God
And donned the gilt-edged robe.

And only Knights who won the day
Were welcomed in the court,
By Kings and Queens who never saw
The battles that they fought.

And Castles on the clifftops
Where allegiances were sworn
Were cold and bitter places
For your ordinary pawn.

It seems those days
Of meek and might
Will always be the same,
For those who play
In black and white
And understand the game.

The Bishop's lost his golden robe,
Stolen by the state,
He sees a world's religions locked
In fundamental hate.

And Knighted politicians win
By kissing under fives,
While sidelined Kings and Queens act out
Their bored symbolic lives.

The Castles now are tower blocks
Without a hint of lawn,
And the lift's still out of order
For your ordinary pawn.

Perhaps those days
Though dim and strange
Will always be the same,
Whoever plays
Can never change
This ancient, puzzling game.

THE WORLD CHESS
CHAMPIONSHIPS,
SADLER'S WELLS
THEATRE
In the main auditorium
nothing happens for long
periods. However, next door in
the studio theatre, experts and
amateurs hypothesise on the
current state of play.

YESTERDAY
We were once just sparkles
in our parents' eyes.

MOTHER

Perhaps this is why you are smiling.
Nurtured by hope, careless of fate, mother to be.
Now, framed by a coffin.

For an instant the joke is on you.
Behind falling shutters of leaves and lids and time
You freeze in a still-life.

Or perhaps you really do still smile.
And we, trapped underground, cannot hear or touch you.
Until the air runs out.

WHOSE HANDS?

*PROTEST AGAINST THE
USE OF PLASTIC BULLETS*
Seamus Duffy, a fifteen-year-old
schoolboy, was hit and killed by a
plastic bullet in Belfast. The
bullets were shot, randomly, from
a Saracen armoured vehicle.

Whose hands
Brought me, struggling,
From womb to bright white room?
No time for tiny finger-patterns to be traced,
A tired disinfected nipple my first taste.
Whose hands slapped me into life?
Not my mother's hands.

Whose hands
Twisted back my wrists,
Chained me to a chair
And cut my feet with broken glass,
Bruised my ribs and tore my hair
Because I was in a different class?
Whose hands scarred my head?
Not my brother's hands.

Whose hands
Let me down,
Didn't believe I was confused
But slipped away half amused
And took my hidden fears to town?
Whose hands let me fall?
Not my lover's hands.

But whose hands built
The walls of gently crafted stone,
And stained the glass and carved the wood
So I can stand alone?
Whose hands, worn and tired,
Died before their time?
Not the Priest's hands.

And whose hands
Built the tombs,
The pyramids of sand,
And concealed the jewels of richer men –
(The Gods who'll one day rise again),
Then spilt their blood, counted the cost,
In case the secrets should be lost?
Not the Pharaoh's hands.

And whose hands
On a Christmas night
Hid nails wrapped tight
Round gelignite beneath the city square?
Whose hands can be so sure
They're right
They've lost the nerve to care?
Not the children's hands.

And whose hands
Within their armour-plated walls
Can etch the street in bullet hails
And carry on as Seamus falls?
My hands? Your hands?
Your brother, your sister, your husband, your wife?
Are these the hands, the very hands, that slap us into life?
The hands that soothe then lie in wait?
Whose hands are these?
Whose hands are these that hold the hate?

Whose hands?

FIRE

standing on the weft
of wet leaves I wait
with thousands of
duffled shadows
chattering with cold
and excitement

it is lit

we feel its primal
glory warm a hint
in ourselves that
we are only surface

our faces glow
with the pleasure
of somewhere knowing
that this is where
we stop

BONFIRE NIGHT,
ISLINGTON
The night of the last great pagan
festival.

SUNDAY **12 NOVEMBER**

AT THE CENOTAPH
In the morning the crowds and
the old soldiers watch the wreath-
laying ceremony. In the afternoon
the National Front pay their own
tribute to the dead.

A.M.
the stoop between his shoulder blades,
the shuffle in his step, the limp
of his stick (wrapped in white
knuckles) do not explain his smile.

rank after rank
after rank after
rank after . . .

is this all that's left?

today the crowd are high on poppies;
like a late guest
I do not trust their inebriation.
why are they clapping?

rank after rank
after rank after
rank after . . .

I cannot see him sixteen and homesick;
I can scarcely see him at all,
smothered by Rule Britannia
in this strangest curtain call.

P.M.
and before that same sun on that same day
has had a chance to set,
the young men march in 4/4 time to drip
the stench of threat.

rank after rank
after rank after
rank after . . .

is this what they left?

and protest's voice is beaten back
beneath the whiplash crack,
as even younger boys in blue
protect the boys in black.

rank after rank
after rank after
rank after . . .

and must hands that stretched to outstretched hands
across a Berlin wall,
fight yet again to overthrow
this sickest curtain call?

FOR JANE

I search for variations on the themes
They taught. Alert and hushed, rich and scared,
I venture where my needs entice my dreams
To reach beyond the score that's been prepared
By those who sing their melodies aloud
At night, frightened by the risk of calm.
I listen for my voice amongst the crowd
And find that only silence holds the charm
That lets me carve a tune, both mine and proud,
That keeps my fragile efforts safe from harm.
And then I learn it's me who lets the shroud
Of discontent remain; 'till on my palm
You trace a soundless stave, too fine to fear,
Where I compose the self I want to hear.

SELF PORTRAIT
With all this looking
around being curious,
it seemed like a good
time to look at
ourselves.

WHEN

When I suck my lover's nipple
She arches her back
And groans.

At once it is complicated.
The pleasure is great
But tinged.

We negotiate a release.
We tease and play
Together.

But my smile is tainted
By the knowledge
Of an end.

We understand too much.
I cannot taste
Only love.

My palate is jaundiced.
It is not a simple
Gift of milk.

Our mature games do not
Permit the world
Of unity.

We cannot be any closer
And yet we feel
The distance.

For unlike the child's smile
We know the cord
Has been cut.

When I suck my lover's nipple
She arches her back
And grieves.

BREAST FEEDING
Sue and Joe

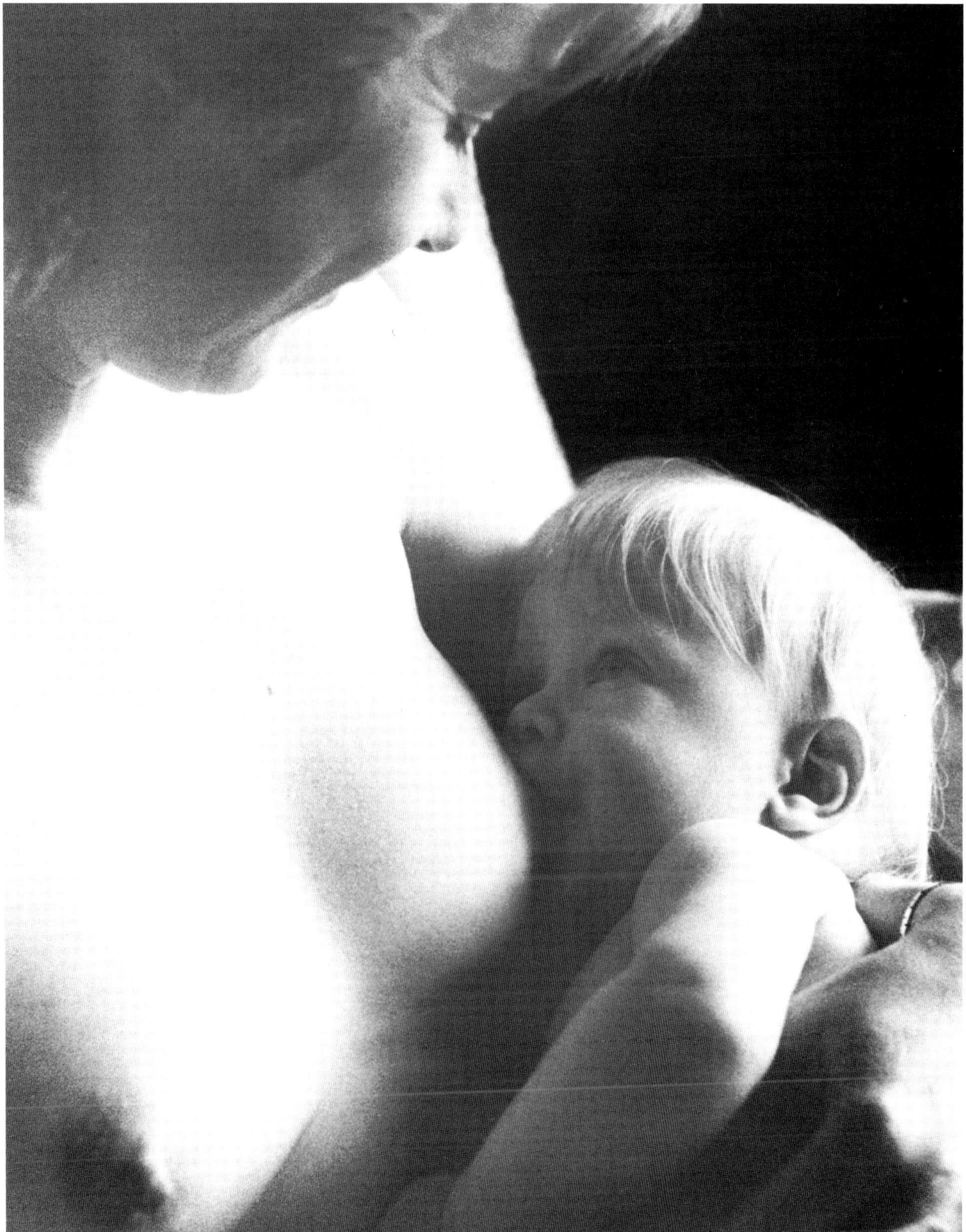

ONE DAY

And one day it will be Christmas.
And we will gather and sing
Around one dead tree.

And one day it will be a Saturday
And we will gather on the terraces
Before jerking to the drum machines.

And when we have found our feet,
We will find that they can only be their own.
Our footsteps must be lonely.

And while she talked to him of love and playgrounds
He wore his Sony Walkman.
We do not even see the same colours.

And one day it will be Easter
And we will argue – "Which came first?
The children or the egg?"

And one day it will be birth day,
And we will snatch at another celebration
Of progress or decay.

And the man down the road says
He wears his face inside out
So he can see more clearly.

And watch the child hesitate before
Placing the round peg in the square hole.
She smiled as it nestled into place.

And just as the pubescent choir boy
Will envy the nightingale,
So I will envy her choice.

And one day it will be raining
And we will gather by her grave
And sing and copulate.

And one day, amongst the hi-fis and TVs
And sweet shops and pay rises and promises
And ideologies and parties,
We will choose ourselves.

HE FINAL PHOTOPOEM

*/e would like to take this
portunity to thank all of the
ty-two weeks for turning up
 time and allowing us to
bble a little in their days....*